DR JEKYLL AND MR HYDE

Have you ever wished to be someone else? Have you ever looked at someone you know and thought, 'He does what he wants. Why shouldn't I do what I want?' And have you then thought that if you looked like someone else, only for one day, you would be free to do anything you wanted? And nobody could blame you for it. Nobody would ever know that it was you, because it wasn't you! How exciting to change into someone else! Just for a day, or perhaps from time to time, not too often. Because if you changed into that other person often, then you might become that other person – and you might find it difficult to be yourself again.

These are dangerous thoughts for someone to have, especially for Doctor Jekyll. Because Doctor Jekyll is a very clever scientist, and he has found a way of turning this dream into reality . . .

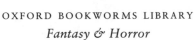

OXFORD BOOKWORMS LIBRARY
Fantasy & Horror

Dr Jekyll and Mr Hyde

Stage 4 (1400 headwords)

Series Editor: Jennifer Bassett
Founder Editor: Tricia Hedge
Activities Editors: Jennifer Bassett and Alison Baxter

ROBERT LOUIS STEVENSON

The Strange Case of
Dr Jekyll
and
Mr Hyde

Retold by
Rosemary Border

OXFORD UNIVERSITY PRESS

OXFORD
UNIVERSITY PRESS

Great Clarendon Street, Oxford OX2 6DP

Oxford University Press is a department of the University of Oxford
It furthers the University's objective of excellence in research, scholarship,
and education by publishing worldwide in

Oxford New York

Auckland Bangkok Buenos Aires Cape Town Chennai
Dar es Salaam Delhi Hong Kong Istanbul Karachi Kolkata
Kuala Lumpur Madrid Melbourne Mexico City Mumbai Nairobi
São Paulo Shanghai Taipei Tokyo Toronto

Oxford and Oxford English are registered trade marks of
Oxford University Press in the UK and in certain other countries

ISBN 0 19 423032 5

This simplified edition © Oxford University Press 2000

Tenth impression 2004

First published in Oxford Bookworms 1991
This second edition published in the Oxford Bookworms Library 2000

A complete recording of this Bookworms edition of *Dr Jekyll and Mr Hyde*
is available on cassette ISBN 0 19 422791 X

Illustrated by Jonathon Heap

Typeset by Hope Services (Abingdon) Ltd
Printed in Spain by Unigraf s.l.

CONTENTS

1

The mysterious door

Mr Utterson the lawyer was a quiet, serious man. He was shy with strangers and afraid of showing his feelings. Among friends, however, his eyes shone with kindness and goodness. And, although this goodness never found its way into his conversation, it showed itself in his way of life. He did not allow himself many enjoyable things in life. He ate and drank simply and, although he enjoyed the theatre, he had not been to a play for twenty years. However, he was gentler towards other men's weaknesses, and was always ready to help rather than blame them. As a lawyer, he was often the last good person that evil-doers met on their way to prison, or worse. These people often carried with them memories of his politeness and fairness.

Mr Utterson's best friend was a distant cousin called

Richard Enfield, who was well known as a fun-loving 'man about town'. Nobody could understand why they were friends, as they were different from each other in every way. They often took long walks together, however, marching through the streets of London in companionable silence.

One of these walks used to take them down a narrow side-street in a busy part of London. It was a clean, busy, friendly street with bright little shops and shiny door-knockers. Near the end of this street, however, stood a dark, mysterious, windowless building. The door had neither bell nor knocker and looked dusty and uncared for. Dirty children played fearlessly on the doorstep, and nobody ever opened the door to drive them away.

One day, as Mr Enfield and his friend passed the building, Mr Enfield pointed to it.

'Have you ever noticed that place?' he asked. 'It reminds me of a very strange story.'

'Really?' said Mr Utterson. 'Tell me.'

'Well,' began Enfield, 'I was coming home about three o'clock on a black winter morning, when suddenly I saw two people. The first was a short man who was walking along the street, and the second was a little girl who was running as fast as she could. Well, the two bumped into each other and the child fell down. Then a terrible thing happened. The man calmly walked all over the child's body with his heavy boots, and left her screaming on the

2

ground. It was an inhuman thing to do. I ran after the man, caught him and fetched him back. There was already a small crowd around the screaming child. The man was perfectly cool, but he gave me a very evil look, which made me feel sick in my stomach. The child's family then arrived, and also a doctor. The child had been sent to fetch the doctor for a sick neighbour, and was on her way home again.

' "The child is more frightened than hurt," said the doctor – and that, you would think, was the end of the story. But, you see, I had taken a violent dislike to the short man. So had the child's family – that was only natural. But the doctor, who seemed a quiet, kindly man, was also looking at our prisoner with murder in his eyes.

'The doctor and I understood each other perfectly. Together we shouted at the man, and told him we would tell this story all over London so that his name would be hated.

'He looked back at us with a proud, black look. "Name your price," he said.

'We made him agree to a hundred pounds for the child's family. With another black look, the man led us to that door over there. He took out a key and let himself into the building. Presently he came out and handed us ten pounds in gold and a cheque for ninety pounds from Coutts's Bank. The name on the cheque was a well-known one.

'I ran after the man, caught him and fetched him back.'

4

' "See here," said the doctor doubtfully, "it isn't usual for a man to walk into an empty house at four in the morning and come out with another man's cheque for nearly a hundred pounds."

' "Don't worry," said the man with an ugly look, "I'll stay with you until the banks open, and change the cheque myself."

'So we all went off, the doctor and the prisoner and myself, and spent the rest of the night at my house. In the morning we went together to the bank. Sure enough, the cheque was good, and the money was passed to the child's family.'

'Well, well,' said Mr Utterson.

'Yes,' said Enfield, 'it's a strange story. My prisoner was clearly a hard, cruel man. But the man whose name was on the cheque was well known all over London for his kind and generous acts. Why would a man like that give his cheque to a criminal?'

'And you don't know if the writer of the cheque lives in that building?' asked Mr Utterson.

'I don't like to ask,' said his friend. 'In my experience, it's not a good idea to ask too many questions, in case the answers are ugly, violent ones. But I've studied the place a little. It doesn't seem like a house. There's no other door, and the only person who uses that door is the man I've just described to you. There are three windows on the side of the house, which look down onto a small courtyard. The windows are shut, but they're always clean. There's a chimney too, which is usually smoking. So somebody must live there.'

The two men continued on their walk. Then Utterson broke the silence.

'Enfield,' he said, 'you're right about not asking too many questions. However, I want to ask the name of the man who walked over the child.'

'Very well,' said Enfield. 'He told us his name was Hyde.'

'What does he look like?'

'He's not easy to describe, although I remember him perfectly. He's a strange-looking man. He's short, but has a strong, heavy body. There's something wrong with his appearance, something ugly and unpleasing – no, something hateful. I disliked him at once.'

Mr Utterson thought deeply. 'Are you sure he used a key?' he asked.

'What do you mean?' asked Enfield in surprise.

'I know it must seem strange,' said his friend. 'But you see, if I don't ask you the name on the cheque, it's because I know it already . . .'

'Well, why didn't you tell me?' said his friend rather crossly. 'Anyway, he did have a key, and he still has it. I saw him use it only a week ago.'

Mr Utterson looked at him thoughtfully, but said nothing more.

In search of Mr Hyde

After dinner that evening Mr Utterson went into his office and unlocked a cupboard. He took out an envelope. It contained the will of Doctor Henry Jekyll, and was written in the doctor's own handwriting.

'If I die, or if I disappear for more than three months,' the will began, 'I wish to leave everything I own to my dear friend Edward Hyde.'

This will had both worried and annoyed Mr Utterson. To a lawyer it was an unusual and dangerous kind of will. It was bad enough when Edward Hyde was only an unknown name, but now that the lawyer knew something about Hyde, the will worried him more than ever. It had seemed like madness before; now it began to seem shameful. With a heavy heart Mr Utterson replaced the envelope in the cupboard, put on his coat and went to see his old friend Doctor Lanyon.

Doctor Lanyon was enjoying his after-dinner coffee. 'Come in, old friend!' he cried. The two men had known each other since their school days. They sat for several minutes, drinking coffee and talking companionably of this and that. At last Mr Utterson mentioned the thoughts that were worrying him.

'I suppose, Lanyon,' he said, 'that you and I are Henry Jekyll's oldest friends?'

'I suppose so,' said Doctor Lanyon, 'but I don't often see him now.'

'Really?' said Mr Utterson in surprise. 'I thought you and he were interested in the same things.'

'We were at one time,' said Doctor Lanyon. 'But more than ten years ago Henry Jekyll became too – well, imaginative for me. He developed some strange, wild, unscientific ideas. I told him so, and I've seen very little of him since then.'

Mr Utterson looked at his friend's red, angry face. 'Only a disagreement about some scientific question,' he thought. 'It's nothing worse than that.' Calmly he continued, 'Did you ever meet a friend of Jekyll's – a man called Hyde?'

'Hyde?' repeated Lanyon. 'No, never.'

Soon the lawyer said goodnight and went home to bed, where he lay awake for a long time thinking about Enfield's description of Hyde, and Doctor Jekyll's will.

Doctor Lanyon and Mr Utterson drank their coffee and talked companionably of this and that.

When at last he fell asleep, he was troubled by dreams. In his mind's eye he saw a faceless man marching over the child's body. Then he saw his old friend Jekyll in bed, while the same faceless figure stood over him. The facelessness of that figure worried him deeply.

'Very well, Mr Hyde,' said the lawyer to himself, 'I will find you, and I will see your face for myself.'

During the next few weeks Mr Utterson spent many hours in the narrow street where Enfield had seen Hyde. He waited patiently near the mysterious door, hoping for a sight of Mr Hyde – and one dry, clear winter night he was successful. The street was empty and silent and small sounds carried a long way. The lawyer heard footsteps. He stepped back into the shadows and waited. A short figure turned the corner and walked towards the mysterious door. Although Mr Utterson could not see his face, he felt a strong, almost violent, dislike for the stranger.

Mr Utterson stepped forward and touched him on the shoulder. 'Mr Hyde?'

'Yes, that's my name,' said the stranger coolly. 'What do you want?'

'I see that you're going in. I'm an old friend of Doctor Jekyll's. My name is Utterson. You must have heard my name – may I come in with you?'

'Doctor Jekyll is not at home,' replied Mr Hyde. 'How did you know me?' he added sharply.

'First let me see your face,' replied the lawyer.

Mr Hyde hesitated for a moment, then he stood under the street light and the lawyer saw his face. 'Thank you,' said Mr Utterson. 'Now I shall know you again. It may be useful.'

'Yes,' said Mr Hyde, 'it may indeed be useful. Here, too, is my address. You may need it one day.' He gave the lawyer his address, which was in a poor part of London.

'Good God!' thought the lawyer, 'does Hyde know about Jekyll's will? Is that what he's thinking of?' But he said nothing.

'And now,' said Mr Hyde, 'how did you know me?'

'You were described to me.'

'Who did that?'

'I know people who know you.'

'Who?' asked Mr Hyde sharply.

'Doctor Jekyll, for example,' said the lawyer.

'He never told you!' cried Mr Hyde in sudden anger. 'Don't lie to me!' And before the lawyer could answer, he turned the key in the lock and disappeared into the house.

Mr Utterson stared at the closed door. 'Why do I dislike him so much?' he said to himself. 'Enfield was right – there is something evil about the man. Poor Henry Jekyll, I'm worried about you. Your new friend will mean trouble for you.'

Round the corner from the narrow street there was a square of handsome old houses. One of these was Doctor Jekyll's house, and Mr Utterson knocked at the front door. The servant answered and told him that Doctor Jekyll was not at home.

'I saw Mr Hyde go in by the laboratory door in the street at the back of the house,' said the lawyer.

'That's right, Mr Utterson,' replied the servant. 'Mr Hyde has his own key, and comes and goes when he likes. We have orders from Doctor Jekyll to obey him.'

Mr Utterson walked home more worried than ever.

A fortnight later Doctor Jekyll gave a dinner party for a few old friends. Mr Utterson was among them and he remained after the others had left.

'I've been wanting to speak to you for some time, Jekyll,' said the lawyer, 'about your will.'

Doctor Jekyll was a tall, well-made man of fifty with a smooth, kindly face. 'My poor friend,' he said, 'you do worry unnecessarily, you know. Like poor Lanyon when I told him about my new ideas. "Imaginative rubbish" he called them . . . I'm very disappointed in Lanyon.'

But the lawyer did not want to talk about Doctor Lanyon. 'You know I've never agreed with your will,' he continued.

'You've told me often enough,' said his friend sharply.

'Well, I've learnt something about your friend Hyde,' continued the lawyer.

The colour of the doctor's handsome face changed from pink to greyish-white. 'I don't want to hear any more,' he said. 'You don't understand. I'm in a very difficult, painful situation.'

'Tell me everything,' said Mr Utterson, 'and I'll do my best to help you.'

'You're very kind, but this is a private matter. I'll tell you one thing – I can get rid of Mr Hyde any time I want. You must understand, however, that I take a great interest in poor Hyde. I know you've seen him – he told me, and I'm afraid he wasn't very polite to you. But I really do care about him. And if anything happens to me, I want you to promise to make sure that he inherits my money.'

'I cannot pretend that I shall ever like him,' said the lawyer.

'I'm not asking you to like him,' said his friend. 'I only ask you to help him, when I'm gone.'

'I promise,' said Mr Utterson sadly.

3

The Carew murder

One night in London, nearly a year later, a servant girl was sitting at her bedroom window, looking out at the moonlit street. She saw a tall, handsome old man with white hair coming along the street, and a shorter, younger man walking towards him. The old man spoke politely to the younger one. He seemed, the girl said later, to be asking his way. Then the girl looked more closely at the younger man and recognized him.

'It was Mr Hyde,' she said later. 'He once visited my master.'

Mr Hyde, the girl said, was carrying a heavy stick. He was playing with it impatiently as he listened to the old man. Then suddenly he seemed to explode with anger.

'He was like a madman,' the servant girl said. 'He shook his stick at the old man, who stepped back in surprise. Then he hit the old man violently with the stick and [knocked him to the ground.] He beat the helpless body again and again. I could hear the bones breaking . . . It was so terrible that I began to feel ill. Then everything went black and I don't remember any more.'

It was two o'clock in the morning before she was conscious again, and able to call the police. The murderer had disappeared, but the dead man was still lying on the ground with the murder weapon beside him. The stick had broken in the middle, and one half still lay beside the murdered man. The police decided that the murderer had carried away the other half. A gold watch and a purse were found in the dead man's pockets, but no cards or papers – except a letter addressed to Mr Utterson.

A policeman brought this letter to the lawyer the next morning. Together they drove to the police station where the body had been taken.

A police inspector showed him the body.

'Yes, I recognize him,' said Mr Utterson heavily. 'He is Sir Danvers Carew.'

'Thank you, sir,' said the inspector. 'And do you recognize this?' He showed Mr Utterson the broken stick and told him the servant girl's story.

Mr Utterson knew the stick at once. 'That's Henry Jekyll's stick!' he said to himself. 'I gave it to him long ago.'

'Is this Hyde a short, evil-looking man?' he asked.

'*Mr Hyde hit the old man violently with the stick and knocked him to the ground.*'

16

'That's how the servant girl described him, sir,' agreed the inspector.

'Come with me,' said Mr Utterson to the inspector. 'I think I know where he lives.'

Mr Utterson led him to the address on Mr Hyde's visiting card. It was in a poor part of London, in a dirty street full of cheap bars and eating-houses. This was the home of Henry Jekyll's favourite friend – the man who would inherit Jekyll's quarter of a million pounds.

An old servant opened the door. Under her silvery hair was a smooth face with a false smile and evil eyes, but she was polite enough.

'Yes,' she said, 'Mr Hyde lives here. But he's not at home. My master came in very late last night. He left again after only an hour.'

'Was that unusual?' asked the inspector.

'Not at all,' replied the servant. 'He's often away, and frequently stays away for months at a time.'

'We would like to see his flat,' said Mr Utterson.

'Oh, I can't do that, sir—' began the servant.

'This gentleman is a police inspector,' said Mr Utterson.

'Ah!' said the servant, looking unnaturally pleased about it, 'Mr Hyde's in trouble! What's he done?'

Mr Utterson and the inspector looked at each other. 'He doesn't seem a very popular person,' said the inspector. He turned to the servant. 'Now please let us in and we'll have a look around.'

Mr Hyde had only two rooms in the house. These were extremely comfortable and in excellent taste, with beautiful pictures on the walls and rich carpets on the floor. Everything was wildly untidy, however, and the fireplace was full of half-burnt papers. Among these the detective found part of a cheque book. He also found the other half of the murder weapon.

'Excellent!' he said. 'Now let's visit the bank and see if they recognize this cheque book.'

Sure enough, the bank held several thousand pounds in an account in the name of Edward Hyde.

'We've got him now, sir,' said the inspector. 'We've got the murder weapon, and we've got his cheque book. Now we only need his description on the "Wanted" notices.'

This was not so easy. There were no photographs of the wanted man and no two people could agree about his appearance. They all agreed on one thing, however. 'An evil man, sir,' the servant girl said. 'You could see it in his face.'

4

Doctor Jekyll receives a letter

Later that same afternoon Mr Utterson found his way to Doctor Jekyll's house. Jekyll's servant, Poole, let him in at once and took him through the kitchen and across the back garden to the laboratory behind the house. It was the first time that Mr Utterson had seen his friend's laboratory, and he looked around curiously.

The old servant led Mr Utterson through the laboratory and up some stairs to the doctor's private study above. This was a large room with tall, glass-fronted cupboards, a large mirror and a big, businesslike table. A good fire burned in the fireplace and beside it sat Doctor Jekyll, looking white and ill. In a thin, tired voice he welcomed his friend.

'Have you heard the news?' said Mr Utterson after the old servant had left.

Beside the fire sat Doctor Jekyll, looking white and ill.

'The newsboys were shouting about it in the street,' Doctor Jekyll said. 'A terrible business.'

'Let me ask you something,' said the lawyer. 'Sir Danvers Carew was my client, but you are my client too, and I want to know what I'm doing. You haven't tried to hide the murderer, have you?'

'Utterson, I promise you,' cried the doctor, 'I promise you I'll never see him again. I've finished with him for ever. And now, indeed, he no longer needs my help. You don't know him like I do. He's safe, quite safe. Believe me, nobody will ever hear of Hyde again.'

The lawyer listened with a serious face. He did not like his friend's feverish, excited look.

'You seem very sure of him,' he replied. 'I hope you're right. If he is caught and comes to trial, your name may be mentioned.'

'I'm absolutely sure of him,' answered Jekyll. 'I can't tell you how I know, but I'm certain. But can you please advise me about one thing? I've received a letter and I don't know whether to show it to the police. May I leave it in your hands, Utterson?'

'You're afraid, I suppose, that the letter will lead the police to Hyde?' asked the lawyer.

'No,' said Doctor Jekyll. 'I don't care what happens to Hyde. I was thinking of my own reputation . . . Anyway, here is the letter.'

It was written in a strange, pointed handwriting and

signed 'Edward Hyde'. 'I am sorry that I have been so ungrateful in the past for your many generous acts,' it began. 'Please don't worry about me. I am quite safe and I am certain that I can escape unharmed whenever I wish.'

'Did this letter come by post?' asked the lawyer.

'No,' replied Doctor Jekyll. 'There was no postmark on the envelope. The letter came by hand.'

'Shall I keep the letter and think about it?' asked Mr Utterson.

'I want you to decide for me,' answered his client. 'I'm not sure of anything any more.'

'Very well,' said the lawyer. 'Now tell me – the part in your will about disappearing for three months or more. Was that Hyde's idea?'

'It was,' whispered Doctor Jekyll.

'He was planning to murder you,' said the lawyer. 'You've had a lucky escape.'

'I've had a lesson too,' said his client, in pain and sadness. 'Oh, what a lesson!' And he covered his face with his hands.⌉

On his way out of the house, the lawyer stopped and spoke to Poole.

'By the way,' he said, 'a letter was handed in today for your master. Who brought it, and what did he look like?'

'Nobody came except the postman, sir,' said the servant in surprise.

'That worries me,' thought Mr Utterson as he walked home. 'Clearly the letter arrived by the laboratory door; perhaps it was even written in the study. I must think about this carefully.'

In the street the newsboys were still shouting, 'Read all about it! Terrible murder!'

The lawyer's thoughts were sad. One of his clients was dead, and the life and reputation of another were in danger. Mr Utterson did not usually ask anyone for advice. Today, however, was different.

That evening he sat by his fireside with his chief clerk, Mr Guest, beside him. The lawyer and his clerk had worked together for many years, and knew and understood each other. Also, Mr Guest had been involved in business with Doctor Jekyll and knew him well.

Outside it was foggy and dark, but the room was bright and warm and there was a bottle of good whisky on the table.

'This is a sad business about Sir Danvers Carew,' said Mr Utterson.

'Yes indeed, sir. The murderer was a madman, of course.'

'I would like your opinion about that,' replied the lawyer. 'I have a letter from the murderer here.'

Mr Guest was interested in the study of handwriting. His eyes brightened at once. 'A murderer's letter!' he said. 'That will be interesting.' He looked carefully at the

The newsboys were still shouting, 'Read all about it!
Terrible murder!'

writing. 'Not a madman, I think,' he said. 'But what unusual handwriting!'

Just then a servant entered with a note.

'Is that note from Doctor Jekyll?' asked Mr Guest. 'I thought I recognized the handwriting. Is it anything private, Mr Utterson?'

'Only an invitation to dinner. Why? Do you want to see the letter?'

'Just for a moment, please, sir.' The clerk put the two letters side by side and studied them carefully. 'Thank you, sir,' he said. 'Very interesting.'

For a moment Mr Utterson hesitated, wondering and worrying. At last he put his thoughts into words. 'Why did you look at the two letters together?' he asked.

'Well, sir, in many ways the two are surprisingly similar.'

'How strange! . . . Mr Guest, I must ask you not to speak of this business to anyone.'

'Of course not, sir,' said the clerk. 'You can depend on me.' Shortly afterwards he said good night to his master and made his way home.

When he was alone, Mr Utterson locked the two letters in his cupboard. 'Well!' he thought. 'So Henry Jekyll wrote that letter for a murderer!' His face was as calm and expressionless as usual, but his heart was filled with fear for his old friend.

5

The death of a friend

Time passed. The search for Mr Hyde continued. Sir Danvers Carew was an important and popular man and the police tried desperately to arrest the murderer and bring him to trial. But there was no sign of Mr Hyde himself, although the police and the newspapers discovered a lot about his past life. Nobody, it seemed, could say one good word about the wanted man. He was a cruel, violent man, who had lived an evil life full of hate and jealousy. None of this, however, was any help to the police. Mr Hyde had just disappeared.

As time went by, Mr Utterson became calmer and more at peace with himself. He was truly sorry that his client, Sir Danvers Carew, was dead, but he was also very glad that Mr Hyde had disappeared. As for Doctor Jekyll, he too appeared calmer and happier. He came out into the world again. He invited friends to his house and accepted invitations to theirs. He had always been a good and generous man. Now, however, he became a churchgoer too. He was busy, he spent a lot of time in the fresh air and he looked happy and carefree. For more than two months he was at peace with himself and the world.

On the 8th of January Mr Utterson was invited to dinner at Doctor Jekyll's house. Doctor Lanyon was there too. 'This is quite like old times,' thought the lawyer as he watched Doctor Jekyll smiling at Doctor Lanyon.

On January 12th, however, and again on the 14th, Doctor Jekyll refused to see visitors.

'The doctor is not well,' explained Poole. 'He hopes you will forgive him, but he cannot see anyone.'

Mr Utterson called again next day, and again the day after that. After two months of almost daily meetings with his old friend, the lawyer felt rather lonely. On the sixth evening he invited his clerk, Mr Guest, to dinner with him, and on the seventh night he went to visit Doctor Lanyon.

Doctor Lanyon made him welcome, but Mr Utterson was shocked by the change in the doctor's appearance. His face, which was usually pink and healthy, was grey and thin, and there was a frightened look in his eyes. He was suddenly an old, sick man.

'He looks', said Mr Utterson to himself, 'like a man who knows he's dying.'

'How are you, Lanyon?' he said. 'You don't look well.'

'I've had a shock, Utterson,' replied Doctor Lanyon. 'And it will cause my death. I have only a few weeks to live.' He paused. 'Well, it comes to us all sooner or later. I've had a good life, on the whole.'

'Jekyll is ill too,' said the lawyer. 'Have you seen him?'

At the name of Jekyll the look on Doctor Lanyon's face changed. 'Please,' he said, holding up a trembling hand, 'don't speak that name in this house.'

'Oh dear,' said Mr Utterson. He hesitated for a moment. 'The three of us have been friends all our lives, Lanyon. We are too old now to make new friends. Can't you forgive and forget? Perhaps I can help?'

'Nothing can be done,' replied Doctor Lanyon. 'Ask him yourself.'

'He won't let me into the house.'

'That doesn't surprise me. One day, Utterson, after I am dead, you will perhaps learn the full story. Meanwhile, if you can sit and talk to me of other things, please stay. Just don't mention that person, as it hurts me to think about him.'

As soon as he got home, Mr Utterson wrote to Doctor Jekyll. In his letter he asked why Jekyll refused to let him into his house, and why he and Doctor Lanyon were no longer friendly. The reply was long and not always easy to understand.

'I'm not angry with our old friend,' Doctor Jekyll

*At the name of Doctor Jekyll the look on Doctor Lanyon's
face changed.*

wrote, 'but I agree with him that the two of us must never meet again. Meanwhile, you must forgive me if from now on I live a very quiet life. If you find my door closed to you, it's because I must travel this dark, dangerous road alone. I have done wrong and I'm being punished for it, and nobody can help me.'

'What is this?' thought Mr Utterson. 'Hyde has disappeared. Jekyll is his normal self again – at least, he was until last week. Has he gone mad?' Then he remembered Doctor Lanyon's words. 'There is something more,' he said to himself, 'something mysterious, but I have no idea what it is.'

A week later Doctor Lanyon was too ill to leave his bed. Two weeks after that he was dead. After his friend's burial, Mr Utterson went home and into his office. From his locked cupboard he took out an envelope, which he had received soon after his friend's death.

In Doctor Lanyon's handwriting he read 'G. J. Utterson. Private.' The lawyer turned the envelope over and over in his hands before he opened it. What terrible news could it contain? With trembling hands Mr Utterson opened the envelope. Inside was another envelope, with the words 'Not to be opened until the death or disappearance of Doctor Henry Jekyll.'

The lawyer could not believe his eyes. 'Death or disappearance' – the words were the same as in Doctor Jekyll's will. 'I understand why Jekyll wrote those words,' said Mr Utterson to himself. 'But why did Lanyon write them too?' For a moment he wanted to open the envelope and uncover the mystery there and then. But Mr Utterson was too honest a man and a lawyer to do that. He knew he must obey his friend's and client's last wish. He locked the envelope away in his cupboard beside Doctor Jekyll's will.

The lawyer was desperately worried about his friend Doctor Jekyll. He was afraid for him too. He called at the house but the doctor always refused to see him.

'How is he, Poole?' Mr Utterson asked the old servant one day.

'Not very well, sir. He spends all his time in the study above his laboratory. He sleeps there as well. He seems very silent and uneasy. Something is worrying him, sir, but he won't tell anyone.'

For a long time the lawyer called almost every day. Little by little, however, he became tired of his friend's refusal to see him, and his visits became less frequent.

6

The face at the window

One Sunday soon afterwards Mr Utterson was walking with his friend Enfield when they happened to pass through the narrow side-street again. Enfield pointed to the mysterious door.

'Well,' he said, 'that story is finished. We shall never see Mr Hyde again.'

'I hope you're right,' said the lawyer. 'Did I tell you? I once saw Hyde too and had the same strong feelings of dislike for him as you did. What an evil man!'

'I agree,' said his friend. 'By the way, why didn't you tell me that our mysterious door led to the laboratory at the back of Doctor Jekyll's house? I didn't know then, but I know now.'

'Well, now that you know, let's go into the courtyard and look up at his window. I must tell you, I'm worried about poor Jekyll. Perhaps the sight of a friendly face will do him good.'

Overhead the evening sky was bright, but the court-yard was cool and dark. At an open window of the study above the laboratory, Doctor Jekyll sat, like a prisoner staring at the world outside.

'I hope you are better, Jekyll,' the lawyer called up to him.

The doctor shook his head sadly. 'I'm not well, Utterson,' he said. 'I shall not be here much longer – thank God.'

'You spend too much time indoors! You ought to get out into the fresh air like Enfield and me . . . By the way, this is my cousin, Mr Enfield . . . Come now – get your hat and join us for a quick walk.'

'You're very kind,' said the doctor. 'But no, it's quite impossible. I would like to invite you and Mr Enfield inside, but the place is not very tidy . . .'

'Well then,' said the lawyer gently, 'we can talk to you from here.'

'That's an excellent idea—' began the doctor, with a smile. But suddenly the smile left his face and was replaced by an expression of hopelessness, fear and horror. The two men below saw it, but only for a second, as the window was shut with a bang. The two men looked at each other, then turned and left the courtyard without a word. In silence they crossed the narrow

'*Come now – get your hat and join us for a quick walk,*'
said Mr Utterson.

side-street. They did not speak until they came out into a busy, noisy street. Then Mr Utterson at last turned and looked at his companion, whose face was as pale as his own. The expression on Doctor Jekyll's face had upset them both deeply.

'God help him!' whispered Mr Utterson. 'God help the poor man!'

But Mr Enfield only nodded his head very seriously and walked on without a word.

7

The last night

It was now March, and Mr Utterson was sitting by the fire after dinner, when he was surprised to receive a visit from Doctor Jekyll's servant, Poole. The old man looked pale and frightened.

'Mr Utterson,' he said, 'something is wrong.'

'Sit down by the fire and tell me all about it.'

'The doctor's locked himself up in his study, sir.'

'That's quite usual, surely,' said the lawyer. 'You know your master's habits as well as I do. He often shuts himself away from the world.'

'Yes, but this time it's different. It frightens me, sir – I've been frightened for more than a week now, and I just can't go on any longer.'

He stopped and stared down at the floor.

'Try and tell me, Poole,' said Mr Utterson gently.

'Something terrible is happening to my master. I can't explain. But . . . please, sir, can you come with me and see for yourself?'

At once Mr Utterson fetched his coat and hat.

'Thank you, sir,' whispered Poole gratefully.

Together they made their way to Doctor Jekyll's house. It was a wild, stormy night. To Mr Utterson the streets seemed strangely empty and lonely. The square, when they reached it, was full of wind and flying dust. The thin trees were blowing wildly, and untidy grey clouds were sailing past a pale, sickly moon.

'Well, sir,' said Poole, 'here we are, and I hope that nothing is wrong.' He knocked softly at the front door. The door was opened just a little and a voice from inside asked, 'Is that you, Poole?'

'Yes – open the door.'

The hall, when they entered, was brightly lit. A good fire was burning. The room was full of people – every servant in the house was there. They looked like a crowd of frightened children.

'What's all this?' said the lawyer. 'What are you all doing here? Your master would not be pleased.'

'They're frightened,' said Poole simply. No one else spoke. A little servant girl began to cry.

'Quiet!' said Poole sharply, trying to control his own fear. 'Now – fetch me a light and we'll finish this business at once. Mr Utterson, sir, please follow me.' He led the way across the back garden towards the laboratory.

'Come as quietly as you can, sir. I want you to hear, but I don't want *him* to hear *you*. And sir — if he asks you to go inside — don't go!'

Mr Utterson's heart gave a little jump of fear, but he bravely followed the servant into the laboratory to the bottom of the stairs.

'Wait here, sir — and listen carefully,' whispered Poole. He himself, again controlling his fear, climbed the stairs and knocked on the study door.

'Mr Utterson would like to see you, sir,' he called.

'Tell him I cannot see anyone,' said a voice from inside the study.

'Thank you, sir,' said Poole. He led Mr Utterson back across the garden and into the house. 'Sir,' he said, 'was that my master's voice?'

The lawyer's face was pale. 'It has changed,' he said.

'Changed? You're right,' said Poole. 'I've worked for Doctor Jekyll for twenty years. That was not my master's voice. Someone has murdered my master. Eight days ago we heard his voice for the last time. "Dear God!" he cried — then no more. The voice you heard just now was the voice of his murderer!'

'This is an extraordinary story, my good man,' said Mr Utterson. He tried hard to appear calm. 'If Dr Jekyll *has* been murdered — why is his murderer still there? What reason could he possibly have for staying?'

'Perhaps you don't believe me, sir, but I know what I heard. For a week now the person – or thing – in that study has been crying night and day for some special chemical powders. My master was in the habit, when he was particularly busy with his scientific work, of writing orders on pieces of paper and leaving them on the stairs. We've had nothing else this week, nothing except written orders and a locked door. I've been to every chemist in town in search of these chemicals of his, but they were never right. They weren't pure enough, he said. I had to take them back to the shop, and try another chemist. I don't know what these chemicals are, but the person in that study wants them terribly badly.'

'Did you keep any of these written orders?' asked Mr Utterson.

Poole reached in his pocket and brought out a note. The lawyer read it carefully. It said: 'I am returning your chemicals, as they are impure and therefore useless. In the year 18— you made up a mixture of chemical powders for Doctor Henry Jekyll. Please search your cupboards for some more of the same mixture and send it to Doctor Jekyll AT ONCE. This is VERY IMPORTANT.'

'This is a strange note,' said Mr Utterson.

'The chemist thought so too, sir,' said Poole. 'When I took him this note, he cried, "All my chemicals are pure, and you can tell your master so!", and he threw the note back at me.'

'Are you sure this is your master's handwriting?' asked Mr Utterson.

'Of course, sir,' said Poole. 'But what does handwriting matter? I've seen my master's murderer!'

'Seen him?' repeated Mr Utterson.

'Yes! It was like this. I came suddenly into the laboratory from the garden. I think he had left the study to look for something. The study door was open and there he was at the far end of the laboratory. He was searching among some old boxes. He looked up when I came in, gave a kind of cry and ran upstairs and into the study. I only saw him for a moment, but my blood seemed to freeze. Sir, if that was my master, why was he wearing a mask over his face? If it was my master, why did he cry out like a trapped animal and run away from me? I've been his servant for twenty years. And then . . .' Poole paused, and covered his face with his hands, too upset to speak.

'This is all very mysterious,' said Mr Utterson, 'but I think I begin to understand. Your master, Poole, is ill. And the illness has changed his appearance. Perhaps that also explains the change in his voice. It certainly explains the mask and the way he has been avoiding his friends. And of course, he's searching for these chemicals because he believes they will make him well again. Dear God, I hope he's right! Poor Jekyll – that is my explanation. It's sad enough, Poole, but it's normal

He looked up, gave a kind of cry and ran upstairs and into the study.

and natural, and there's nothing to be alarmed about.'

'Sir,' said the servant, 'that . . . thing was not my master. My master is a tall, fine, well-built man. The stranger was much shorter . . . Sir, I have been with my master for twenty years and I know his appearance as well as I know my own. No, sir, that thing in the mask was never Doctor Jekyll, and I believe that he – it – murdered my master!'

'Poole,' said the lawyer, 'if you say that, I must make sure. We must break down the study door.'

'You're right, Mr Utterson!' cried the old servant.

'Very well. Will you help me? If we are wrong, I'll make sure that you're not blamed for it.'

'There's an axe in the laboratory,' suggested Poole.

'You realize, Poole,' said Mr Utterson, 'that this may be dangerous for us both? Let us now be honest with each other. This masked figure that you saw – you're certain that it was not your master.'

'That's right, sir.'

'Did you in fact recognize it?'

'Well, sir, it was all so quick that I'm not really sure. But – well, I think it was Mr Hyde. It was short, like Mr Hyde, and it moved in the same light, quick, active way. And who else could come in by the laboratory door from the street? You must remember, sir, that at the time of the Carew murder Mr Hyde still had the laboratory key with him. But that's not all.

Mr Utterson, did you ever meet Mr Hyde?'

'Yes,' replied the lawyer. 'I once spoke with him.'

'Then you will know, sir, that there is something strange about Mr Hyde, something evil.'

'I agree with you,' said Mr Utterson. 'I felt something like that, too.'

'Yes, sir. Well, when that thing in the mask jumped out from behind the boxes and ran up the stairs, I had exactly the same feeling. That thing behind the mask was Mr Hyde!'

'I understand, Poole, and I believe you,' said the lawyer slowly. 'And I believe poor Henry Jekyll has been murdered. I believe too that his murderer is still hiding in the study. Now, Poole, let's go and make an end of it.'

Together they went out into the back garden. The clouds had covered the moon and it was now quite dark. As they passed silently by the wall of the laboratory, they stopped and listened. Further away they could hear the everyday noises of a London evening. From the study above them, however, came the sound of footsteps moving backwards and forwards across the floor.

'It walks like that all day, sir,' whispered Poole, 'yes, and most of the night too. It only stops when some more chemicals arrive from the chemist. Ah, sir, listen to that – do you think those are my master's footsteps?'

The short, light steps were indeed very different from Henry Jekyll's long, heavy ones.

'Have you anything else to tell me, Poole?' asked the lawyer heavily.

'Once,' said Poole, 'I heard it weeping.'

'Weeping?' repeated Mr Utterson in horror.

'Weeping like a lost child,' said the old servant. 'It tore my heart. I felt like weeping too.'

'Well,' said the lawyer, 'we have a job to do.'

They went into the laboratory and climbed the stairs to the study. 'Jekyll,' called the lawyer in a loud voice, 'I must see you.' He paused for a moment, but there was no reply. 'If you refuse to let me in, then I'll break down the door!'

'Utterson,' said a voice from inside the study, 'I beg you to leave me alone!'

'That's not Jekyll's voice!' shouted Mr Utterson. 'It's Hyde's! Break the door down, Poole!'

The axe rose and fell. The door shook and a scream of pure fear, like a trapped animal, rang from the study. Again the axe crashed against the door. But the wood was strong and the lock was well made. At last, however, the door fell inwards upon the carpet.

The two men stared into the study. They saw a warm, comfortable room with a good fire burning in the fireplace and a few papers on the big table. A friendly, homely room. But face down in the middle of the floor there lay the body of a man. The lawyer turned it over on its back and saw the face of Edward Hyde. He was

Face down in the middle of the floor there lay the body of a man.

dressed in clothes that were much too large for him, and in his hand he held a small bottle.

The lawyer shook his head. 'He's taken poison, Poole,' he said. 'I fear we've come too late to save Doctor Jekyll, and too late to punish his murderer too. Now we must find your master's body.'

They searched everywhere, but there was no sign of Henry Jekyll, dead or alive.

'Perhaps your master has escaped,' said Mr Utterson hopefully. He went to check the door from the laboratory into the narrow side-street. It was locked, and covered with dust. On the floor nearby he found a broken key.

'It's a long time since anyone opened this door!' said Mr Utterson.

'Yes,' said Poole, picking up the broken key. 'So how did Hyde get in?'

'This is too difficult for me, Poole,' said the lawyer. 'Let's go back to the study.'

They searched the study again. 'Look, sir,' said Poole, pointing to a small table in the corner. There were bottles of liquid and some white powders lying in saucers. 'He was testing his chemicals here.'

One of the doctor's books was lying on the floor. Its cover was torn off. The lawyer picked it up. Doctor Jekyll loved his books and always took great care of them. But he had written all over this one – the handwriting was un-mistakable – before tearing it and throwing it on the floor.

Then the lawyer noticed the tall mirror on the wall between the glass-fronted bookshelves.

'How strange,' said Mr Utterson. 'Why did Jekyll want a mirror in his study?'

Next they turned to the desk and found a large packet addressed to Mr Utterson. The handwriting was Doctor Jekyll's. The lawyer opened the packet and three envelopes fell out on to the floor. The first contained a will. It was like Doctor Jekyll's first will in every way – except one. The doctor had left all his money, not to Edward Hyde, but to Gabriel John Utterson.

The lawyer looked at the will, then at Poole, and finally at the dead man on the floor.

'I just don't understand,' he whispered. 'Hyde has been here all this time – why didn't he destroy this will?'

He picked up the next envelope. It contained a short note in the doctor's handwriting. Mr Utterson saw the date. 'Poole!' he cried, 'this is today's date on the letter. Jekyll was alive here today. He can't be dead – he has run away or is hiding somewhere. And if so, why? If he's alive, can we be sure that Hyde killed himself? We must be careful, Poole, or we may involve your master in some terrible danger.'

'Why don't you read the note, sir?' asked the servant.

'Because I'm afraid,' said the lawyer, in a worried voice. Slowly, he lifted the letter, and read:

My dear Utterson,

If you are reading this, it means that I have disappeared. Please go home and read Lanyon's letter. Afterwards, please read the confession of

Your unfortunate and unhappy friend,

Henry Jekyll

'This must be the confession,' said Mr Utterson to himself, picking up the third and largest envelope. He put it in his pocket. 'Say nothing about these papers, Poole,' he said. 'If your master has died or disappeared, this paper may save his reputation. It's now ten o'clock. I must go home and study these papers in peace and quiet. But I shall come back here before midnight, and then we shall send for the police.'

They went out, locking the laboratory door behind them. With a heavy heart Mr Utterson walked home to read his letters.

8
Doctor Lanyon's letter

Dear Utterson,

Four days ago, on the 9th of January, I received a letter by
the evening post. It was in the handwriting of my old friend
Henry Jekyll. I was rather surprised, as we were not in the
habit of writing to each other, and I had had dinner with him
the night before. When I came to read the letter, I was even
more surprised. The letter said:

Dear Lanyon,

You are one of my oldest friends. Although we have
sometimes disagreed on scientific matters, I have always
remained your friend. I would do anything for you, Lanyon –
please will you do something for me now?

Please, old friend, come to my house at once with this
letter in your hand. Poole, my servant, has his orders. He

will be here with a locksmith. Break the lock of my study door, and then you must go in there alone. Open the glass-fronted cupboard on the left-hand side and look on the fourth shelf from the top. On it you will find some packets of chemical powders, a small bottle and a book. Please take everything back to your house.

If you leave as soon as you receive this letter, you should be back home before midnight. At that time you will receive a visit from a man. Please give him the bottle, the powders and the book, and I shall always be grateful to you.

Do not fail me, Lanyon. Believe me, my life and my peace of mind depend on you. I am in fearful danger and only you can save me.

Your friend,
Henry Jekyll

After reading this letter, I was sure that Doctor Jekyll was mad. But a friend is a friend, and so I went at once to his house. Jekyll's servant had received by the same post a letter similar to mine, and he was waiting for me with the locksmith. Together we went through the old laboratory and climbed the stairs to the doctor's private study. The door was very strong, with an excellent lock, but the locksmith knew his job. Soon the door stood open and I entered the study. I opened the cupboard and found the shelf. Sure enough, the powders, the bottle and the book were there, and I took them home with me.

At home I looked at everything more carefully. There were several packets of white powder and a bottle of red, strong-smelling liquid. The book contained nothing except a list of dates, going back several years. The last date was nearly a year ago. Here and there the doctor had added a few words. The word 'double' appeared very early in the list, followed by the word 'Failed!!'. 'Double' appeared in the list several more times . . . What was Jekyll doing? The book looked like a list of unsuccessful experiments. How could I, by taking these things to my house, save my friend's life and peace of mind? And what was the reason for this midnight visitor? I put my old gun in my pocket, then I put everything in a box for my midnight visitor to collect.

At midnight exactly there was a knock on my door. A short man was standing in the shadows.

'Are you from Doctor Jekyll?' I asked. He bent his head. Although I could not see his face, there was something unpleasing about him and I was glad I had a weapon. I invited him into the house and there, in the bright light, I took a closer look at him.

His appearance was extremely strange. His clothes were well made and expensive, but they were far too large for him. He looked like a child wearing his father's clothes, but there was nothing childlike about this man. He was short, as I have said, but very strong. At the same time there was a look of sickness and horror about him, and his face was a mask of pain, violence and hate. As a doctor I could perhaps feel sorry

51

for him; as a man I felt only fear and dislike.

'Have you got it?' said the stranger impatiently, reaching out his hand and touching my arm. His touch made my blood run cold. I shook off his hand. 'Come, sir,' I said calmly. 'Sit down and introduce yourself.'

'I apologize, Doctor Lanyon,' the stranger said more politely. 'Doctor Henry Jekyll sent me here on an important matter. I have to collect something from you.'

I gave him the box. He took it with trembling hands. 'At last!' he cried. He turned to me. His face was deathly pale. 'Have you a medicine glass?' he asked.

I gave it to him. He put a little of the red liquid in the glass and added a packet of powder. A small cloud of smoke rose from the glass and the colour of the liquid changed from red to purple, and from purple to a watery green. The stranger put the glass down on the table and looked sharply at me.

'And now,' he said, 'choose carefully. You can leave the room now. Or you can stay and experience something new, something unknown to science. You can be rich, famous and successful, if only you will believe.'

'Sir,' I said, trying to remain calm, 'I don't understand what you're trying to say, and I think you are probably mad. But I will stay.'

'Very well,' said the stranger. 'Now remember your promise. You've been an unbeliever all your life. You laughed at Doctor Jekyll's ideas and called them unscientific rubbish – now see for yourself!'

*He put a little of the red liquid in the glass and
added a packet of powder.*

He put the glass to his lips and drank the liquid. His whole body shook and jumped and he almost fell. He held onto the edge of the table, breathing fast through his open mouth. As I watched, his whole body seemed to change. He seemed to become taller, fatter – his face turned black and its shape began to change . . . The next moment I jumped back against the wall, trembling with fear and horror. There before my eyes, pale and shaken and sick, stood Henry Jekyll!

I cannot make myself write down the things that Jekyll, with tears in his eyes, confessed to me that night.

Now fear and horror are my only companions. Sleep has left me and I feel that I have not long to live. As I write, I wonder. Did I imagine it all? As a scientist I cannot believe it – but I saw it happen with my own eyes.

I will say just one thing more, Utterson. The evil thing that came into my house that night – as Jekyll told me – was known by the name of Hyde, and was wanted by the police for the murder of Sir Danvers Carew.

Hastie Lanyon

With fear in his heart, Mr Utterson put away Doctor Lanyon's letter, and then opened the confession of Doctor Henry Jekyll.

9

Doctor Jekyll's confession

I was born in the year 18—. I inherited a large
fortune, a strong healthy body and an excellent mind.
I was naturally hard-working and soon I was extremely
successful in my chosen work as a scientist. Although I
was still young, important people came to me for advice.
At an age when most young men are going out and
having fun, I was behaving like a grey-haired old
man.

This was not easy for me. The outside world saw
a serious, hard-working doctor. Behind this quiet
character, however, was an active, fun-loving young
man-about-town. This, of course, was nothing to be
ashamed of, but I did not realize that at the time. I was
ashamed, and I soon learned to keep my two lives
separate.

I spent many hours in my laboratory, searching for the right mixture of chemicals to make my drug.

I was not dishonest in any way. Both these people were me. The serious, successful young doctor was me, and the wild, fun-loving, irresponsible young man was me too. I thought about this for a long time and slowly I realized that I was not extraordinary in this. Every man has two sides to his character. He is two people. They live together – often uncomfortably – in the same body.

'How fantastic,' I thought, 'if I could separate these two characters and give my fun-loving side his freedom. Then he could go out and enjoy himself unashamedly and leave serious, studious Doctor Jekyll to get on with his important, life-saving work.'

'Was it possible,' I wondered, 'to find a drug that could give each side of my character its own separate face and body?'

After much thought and careful study I believed I had found the answer. I had read many scientific books and spent many hours in my laboratory, searching for the right mixture of chemicals to make my drug. At last I had everything I needed except a special kind of salt. I bought some from a chemist, and then I was ready.

I hesitated for a long time before I began my experiment. Only a small mistake in the mixture of the drug could mean immediate death. But in the end, my wish to know was stronger than my fear. And so, late one disastrous night, I mixed everything together and prepared my drug. I watched the smoke rising from the liquid as it changed colour from red to purple and at last to green. Then, bravely, I drank every bitter drop.

I felt a violent sickness in my stomach and a terrible pain in all my bones. The room seemed to turn round and round and I trembled with fear. Then the fear and pain disappeared and a strange, sweet feeling took its place. Wild thoughts danced through my mind. They were not good, serious thoughts. They were the wild passions of an evil and cruel stranger. But inside myself I felt younger, lighter, more carefree than ever before. 'If this is pure evil,' I thought, 'I like it.'

I stood there, enjoying these strange new thoughts and passions – and suddenly realized that I was shorter. At that time there was no mirror in my study. Later I put one on the wall of my study so that I could watch these changes in my appearance. Now, however, it was three o'clock in the morning and all the servants were asleep. I decided it was safe to go to my bedroom in my new body and take a look at myself in the mirror there. I crossed the garden and entered my house like a stranger. As I came into my room, I saw Edward Hyde for the first time.

At that time, the good side of my character was stronger than the evil side. Henry Jekyll had his faults, but he was mostly a good, kind man. I cannot be sure, but I believe that is the reason why Edward Hyde was so much smaller than Henry Jekyll. But that was not the only difference between the two men. Henry Jekyll had a kind, open, honest face. Pure evil stared out of Edward Hyde's eyes. I felt no dislike, however. Indeed, I welcomed him. Edward Hyde was me, young and strong and full of life.

Later, however, I noticed that Hyde's appearance and manner had a strong effect on other people. Nobody could meet Edward Hyde without a feeling of dislike and horror. I believe I understand the reason for this too. Everyone is a mixture of good and evil. Even the worst criminal has a little good in him. Only Edward Hyde was pure evil.

I stood for a long time, staring at the mirror. 'Am I trapped?' I wondered. 'If I am, I must leave this house before daylight. If I don't, I shall be arrested as a thief.'

I hurried back to my study. With trembling hands I mixed another dose of the drug and drank it. Again I felt that terrible pain and sickness, but a few seconds later I found myself with the face and body and character of Henry Jekyll once more.

I blame myself for the things that happened later. It was not the fault of the drug. That was neither good nor evil. But it opened the prison doors and allowed Edward Hyde to escape. Soon he was out of control.

He, you will remember, was wholly evil. Doctor Jekyll was not wholly good, however. He was a normal man with normal faults and weaknesses, and Hyde was too strong for him.

I welcomed Hyde, therefore. I arranged everything very carefully. I bought a flat in a poor part of London, where I kept Hyde's clothes and employed a servant to do the housework. I took a dose of the drug whenever I wanted to forget my old, quiet, serious self for a time. In those early days – God forgive me! – I thought it was all very amusing. Doctor Jekyll was well known. Nobody knew Hyde, however, and in his body I was free to do as I wished.

I will not go into details about my adventures and shameful acts as Hyde. Jekyll remained as good and kind as ever and always did his best to undo the harm that Hyde did. But as time went by, Jekyll became less and less able to control Hyde.

One night Hyde injured a child in the street and a passer-by saw him. That passer-by was your cousin. I recognized him when the two of you came to my window. Your cousin caught Hyde and an angry crowd collected. They asked for money for the child's family. In the end, in order to escape, Hyde had to give your cousin a cheque in the name of Jekyll.

I learned my lesson from this, and opened a new bank account in the name of Hyde. I even gave Hyde different handwriting. I was sure I was safe – but I was wrong.

Two months before the murder of Sir Danvers Carew I went out on one of my evil adventures. Before I went to bed, I took a dose of the drug and became Doctor Jekyll once more. I woke up in bed the next morning with a strange feeling that something was wrong . . . I looked around the room, then down at my hand. Henry Jekyll's hand was large, white, and well-made, but the hand I saw that morning on the bedcover was thin, bony, greyish-brown, and hairy. It was the hand of Edward Hyde.

Sick with horror, I stared at it. 'I was Henry Jekyll when I went to bed,' I thought. 'And now I am Edward Hyde . . . What possible explanation can there be? And, more important, how can I get to my study and take the drug?'

Then I realized that the servants were quite used to the comings and goings of Hyde. I put on Hyde's clothes and marched confidently through the house. Poole stared in surprise to see Mr Hyde so early in the morning, but I did not care. Ten minutes later Doctor Jekyll had returned to his own shape and was sitting down, pretending to eat breakfast.

Too worried to eat, I sat there thinking hard about my situation. I realized that in recent weeks Hyde had become bigger and stronger, both in body and character.

It was the hand of Edward Hyde.

'What will I do,' I thought, 'if Hyde takes control?' I thought about the drug. Once, in the early days, it had failed completely, and sometimes I had had to take a double dose before I changed into Hyde. Now, however, it was quite easy to become Hyde – the problem was to become Jekyll again after my adventures. My good self and my evil self were fighting for my mind and body – and my evil self was winning.

I knew I had to choose between the two, and I chose Doctor Jekyll. Perhaps I was not wholly serious about this, however, because I did not sell Hyde's flat or destroy his clothes. For two months I lived the life of a quiet and responsible man. But soon I began to miss Hyde – his strong young body, his love of life and his dark adventures in the narrow, nameless streets of London. One night, when my life as Jekyll seemed impossibly dull and boring, I mixed a dose of the drug and drank it.

It was like opening the door of a cage and letting a wild animal escape. That night I became a madman, and beat Sir Danvers to death – for no reason at all. I felt only a wild delight as I hit his body again and again. Afterwards I ran to the flat and destroyed all my papers. I was not ashamed of my crime. Instead I was filled with a high, sweet excitement. I relived the murder as I walked back home through the streets. I felt strong and masterful . . . Edward Hyde had a song on his lips as he mixed a dose of the drug. 'Your very good health, Sir Danvers!' he laughed as he drank. A moment of terrible pain, then poor Henry Jekyll fell to his knees and begged God to forgive him.

When I was myself again, I locked the door that led from the street to my laboratory. I broke the key and threw it away. 'Goodbye for ever, Mr Hyde!' I whispered.

The next day the news of the murder was all over London. The servant girl had seen the crime and recognized Mr Hyde. My other self was wanted by the police.

In some ways I was glad. Now Hyde could not show his face to the world again. If he did, every honest man in London would be proud to report him to the police.

Once again I led a busy, responsible and almost happy life . . . until one fine, clear January day. I was sitting on a seat in the park, enjoying the sunshine, when suddenly I felt deathly sick. I began to tremble all over. Soon, however, I felt well again – not only well, but young, strong and fearless. I looked down; my clothes were suddenly too big, the hand on my knee was the bony, hairy hand of Edward Hyde. It was so sudden. One moment I was a famous and popular doctor, the next I was a violent criminal who was wanted for murder.

How could I get to my study to take the drug? I had locked the street door to my laboratory and broken the key. I could not, therefore, enter from the street. I could not go in through the house because of the servants. I needed help from outside. I thought of Lanyon, but how could I reach him? And how could I persuade him to let Hyde into his home? How, too, could I persuade him to break into Doctor Jekyll's private study? It looked impossible.

Then I remembered. My appearance was unrecognizable, but my handwriting was unchanged. I could still write a letter in Doctor Jekyll's name! Calling a passing taxicab, I ordered the driver to drive to a hotel quite near Lanyon's house. Of course Jekyll's clothes were much too large for my body, and I had trouble in climbing into the cab. The driver noticed my strange appearance and could not help laughing. I gave him such a black look, however, that the smile froze on his face. In my desperate fear and danger, I was like a pain-maddened animal, ready to kill or wound at any moment. I wanted to pull the driver from his seat and murder him then and there. But I was clever too. My life depended on my coolness, and I fought to control my murderous passions.

We reached the hotel. I paid the driver and went inside, holding up my too-large trousers. The servants smiled when they saw my strange appearance. I stared angrily at them and their smiles disappeared at once. I gave my

The servants smiled when they saw my strange appearance.

orders and they led me to a private room and brought me some writing paper and a pen.

Hyde in danger of his life was a new experience for me. He – I write 'he' because I find it hard to write 'I' – he was not human. His only feelings at that time were fear and hate. Hyde was wholly evil, but he was not stupid. He knew that his life depended on two letters, one to Lanyon and one to Poole. If he failed, he would die.

Carefully he wrote the letters and sent a servant to post them. After that he sat all day by the fire in the private room. There too he had dinner, brought by a frightened waiter. At last, when darkness had covered the city, he sat in the corner of a closed taxicab. 'Just drive round!' he ordered, and the driver drove backwards and forwards through the streets of London.

Then, when Hyde thought the driver was beginning to suspect something, he sent the taxicab away and continued on foot. He was a strange figure in his too-large clothes, with fear and hate staring out of his eyes. He walked along talking to himself. Once a woman spoke to him.

'Will you buy my matches, sir?' she begged. Hyde hit her across the face, and she ran away in fear.

My plan was successful. And when I arrived in Lanyon's house, I took the dose of the drug that returned me to my normal appearance.

Immediately afterwards I felt deeply ashamed. Perhaps it was Lanyon's horror that made me feel like that. I do not know. But I hated myself and I was conscious of an important change in my feelings. I was no longer afraid of the police – I was afraid of Hyde himself. The thought of his short, strong, hairy body and his evil, cruel, wholly selfish mind filled me with horror.

Exhausted by the horrors of that day, I slept heavily. I woke in the morning feeling weak and shaky, but quite normal. I still hated and feared the thought of the wild animal inside me, and I had not forgotten the desperate dangers of the day before. But I was at home and close to my drugs, and I was most deeply grateful for my escape.

I was walking across the garden after breakfast, enjoying the clear wintry air, when suddenly my body was again torn by those indescribable feelings which I always experienced after a dose of the drug. I only just reached my study before I was again burning and freezing with the violent passions of Hyde. With feverish speed I mixed the drug. This time I had to take a double dose to return to my old shape. And then, only six hours later, the pains returned and I had to repeat the dose.

From that day onwards the situation worsened. I needed larger and more frequent doses in order to stay in Jekyll's body. The pains came unexpectedly, but most of all when I was asleep. I was afraid to go to bed, or even to sleep for a few moments in my chair. If I did so, I always woke as Hyde.

Soon Jekyll was a sick man, feverish and weakened by

pain and fear. As Jekyll grew weaker, Hyde became stronger than ever. He burned with hate for everybody and everything. And Hyde and Jekyll now hated each other with equal passion. Jekyll hated Hyde because Hyde was evil and inhuman, and because Hyde was stronger than he was. Jekyll lived in fear of waking up and finding himself in Hyde's body, with all Hyde's evil passions. Hyde hated Jekyll for a different reason. His fear of death – the punishment for murder – drove him to the hiding-place of Jekyll's body. But he hated this prison and was always fighting to escape from Jekyll's mind and body, and take control. He also hated Jekyll's weakness and his sad, hopeless condition. Most of all, he hated Jekyll's dislike of him. This was why Hyde sometimes did things to annoy Jekyll. He tore the doctor's books and wrote all over them. He burned his letters and even destroyed a picture of the doctor's dead father.

Only Hyde's fear of his own death stops him from killing me. His love of life is terribly strong, and he knows that if he kills me, he too will die. I almost feel sorry for him.

It is useless to continue this confession. The final disaster has arrived, and will put an end to my punishment. I shall soon lose my own face and character for ever. I have only a few doses of the drug left. I sent Poole to the same chemist to fetch some more chemicals. When he brought them, I mixed a dose of the drug. The liquid smoked and changed from red to purple, but it did not turn green. I drank it, and looked in the mirror. But there was no effect. Edward Hyde's face still stared back at me.

I expect Poole has told you that I have searched London for the chemicals I need. It is no good. I have decided that the first chemicals I bought were not absolutely pure. By accident, they contained something unknown to myself or to the chemist that prepared them. And that unknown something made my drug effective. So my drug was an accidental discovery that cannot be repeated.

About a week has passed. I have used the last of the old chemicals, and for the moment I am Henry Jekyll again. But I cannot write much more – I have very little time. If Hyde returns while I am writing this confession, he will tear it to pieces to annoy me. If I finish it, however, he will probably not notice it. He lives only for the moment, and he is already a changed man. He is like a trapped animal now. He sits in my chair trembling and weeping with hate and fear. All the time he listens for the policeman's knock at the door. Will he be caught at last, and put to death? Or will he be brave enough to take a dose of poison at the last moment?

Well, that is not my business. This is the true hour of my death. When you read this, the Henry Jekyll you know will be dead. The rest of the story is about Edward Hyde. Now, as I put down my pen, I bring the life of unhappy Henry Jekyll to an end.

For the moment I am Henry Jekyll again. But I cannot write much more — I have very little time.

GLOSSARY

account *(n)* when you keep your money in a bank, you have a
 bank account

appearance what someone or something looks like

axe a heavy stick with a sharp piece of metal on the end; used
 for cutting down trees

burial burying; putting a dead body in a grave in the ground

cage a box or a place with bars for keeping wild animals

chemical *(n)* liquid or solid things used in or made by chemistry

client someone who pays another person (e.g. a lawyer, a
 builder) to do a job for him

confession saying that you have done something wrong

courtyard an unroofed open space surrounded by walls or
 buildings

dose *(n)* how much medicine you take at one time

drug *(n)* a chemical mixture that can make sick people well (a
 medicine), or that can harm people's minds and bodies

evil very bad; harmful

experiment *(n)* a scientific test on something in order to find
 out what happens and to learn something new

forgive to stop being angry with someone about something

God the 'person' who made the world and controls all things

Good God! an expression of surprise or fear

laboratory a room where scientists work and do experiments

liquid anything that flows and is not a gas; oil and water are
 liquids

locksmith a person who makes and mends locks

mask a cover worn over the face to hide it

master an old-fashioned word for a male employer

memory   something that you remember
mind *(n)*   the part of the head that thinks, feels and remembers
mix *(v)*   to put different things together
mixture   the result when different things are mixed together
pale   with little colour in the face
passion   a strong feeling of hate, love, or anger
poison *(n)*   something that can kill you if it is eaten or drunk
pure   completely clean, not mixed with anything else
reputation   what people think or say about someone else
respectable   thought to be good, correct, etc., by other people
science   the study of natural things, e.g. biology, chemistry
scientific   of or belonging to science
scientist   a person who studies science, or works with science
servant   someone who is paid to work in another person's house
shameful   very bad or wrong; causing unhappy, painful feelings
shock *(n)*   a sudden and very unpleasant surprise
thought *(n)*   something that you think
upset *(adj)*   unhappy or worried about something
weak   not strong
weep   to cry
will *(n)*   someone's written wishes that say who will inherit their
   money after they die

Dr Jekyll and Mr Hyde

ACTIVITIES

Before Reading

1 Read the back cover and the story introduction on the first page of the book. What can you guess about this story? Circle Y (yes) or N (no) for each ending.

1 Dr Jekyll finds a way to change into another person . . .
   a) and change back into himself again. Y/N
   b) but can't change back again. Y/N

2 Dr Jekyll changes into another person . . .
   a) to do good things. Y/N
   b) to do bad things. Y/N

3 Mr Hyde is . . .
   a) someone who hates Dr Jekyll. Y/N
   b) another scientist who helps Dr Jekyll with his experiments. Y/N

2 Imagine that you could change into another person for a time. Which of these people would you choose, and why?

1 A man (if you are a woman) or a woman (if you are a man).
2 A person who is much older or younger than you are.
3 A person who is very rich.
4 A person who doesn't have to work or to do anything except enjoy himself.
5 A person whose job is very different from yours.
6 A person who is famous all over the world.

While Reading

Read Chapters 1 and 2. Are these sentences true (T) or false (F)? Rewrite the false ones with the correct information.

1 The child that Mr Hyde walked over was badly hurt.
2 Mr Enfield hated Mr Hyde as soon as he saw him.
3 Mr Utterson knew whose name was on the cheque.
4 Mr Utterson first heard of Mr Hyde in Mr Enfield's story about him.
5 Dr Jekyll's will left everything to Dr Lanyon.
6 Dr Lanyon agreed with Dr Jekyll's scientific ideas.
7 Mr Hyde had his own key and could come and go in Dr Jekyll's house when he liked.
8 Dr Jekyll told Mr Utterson all about Mr Hyde.

Read Chapters 3 and 4. Who said these words, and to whom? Who, or what, were they talking about?

1 'I gave it to him long ago.'
2 'My master came in very late last night.'
3 'We've got him now, sir.'
4 'Have you heard the news?'
5 'I've finished with him for ever.'
6 'But can you please advise me about one thing?'
7 'You've had a lucky escape.'
8 'Who brought it, and what did he look like?'
9 'Well, sir, in many ways the two are surprisingly similar.'

Read Chapters 5 and 6. Then choose the best word to complete this passage. (Use one word for each gap.)

The police could not _____ Mr Hyde because he had _____. For two months things seemed normal, and then Dr Jekyll suddenly _____ to see visitors. Dr Lanyon became _____, and told Mr Utterson not to _____ Dr Jekyll's _____ in his house. Then Dr Lanyon _____ and left Mr Utterson an _____, which was not to be opened until the _____ or _____ of Dr Jekyll. One day Mr Utterson saw Dr Jekyll at his window, and the _____ of hopelessness on his friend's face _____ him deeply.

Before you read Chapter 7, can you guess what happens next? Choose some of these ideas.

1 Mr Hyde returns to Dr Jekyll's house.
2 Mr Hyde keeps Dr Jekyll prisoner in his own house.
3 Dr Jekyll murders Mr Hyde.
4 Mr Hyde murders Dr Jekyll.
5 Mr Utterson and Poole break down Dr Jekyll's study door and find a dead body.
6 Your own idea.

Read Chapter 7, and then answer these questions.

1 What had Poole heard in the study?
2 What did Mr Utterson and Poole find in the study?
3 What was in the packet addressed to Mr Utterson?
4 What two things about the will were surprising?
5 What did the note ask Mr Utterson to do?

Read Chapter 8. Then put these parts of sentences into the right order, and join them to make a short paragraph.

1 to give these things to a man who . . .
2 after he had mixed the chemicals and a liquid in a glass, . . .
3 In January Dr Lanyon received a letter from Dr Jekyll, . . .
4 Then the stranger drank the liquid and . . .
5 would come to his home at midnight.
6 asking him to collect some chemicals, a bottle, and a book from Dr Jekyll's house and . . .
7 changed into Dr Jekyll in front of Dr Lanyon's eyes.
8 he invited Dr Lanyon to stay and experience something unknown to science.
9 At midnight a strange, evil-looking man arrived, and . . .

Read Chapter 9, and then answer these questions.

Why

1 . . . did Dr Jekyll want to separate the two sides of his character?
2 . . . did people feel dislike and horror on meeting Hyde?
3 . . . did it become harder and harder to change back into Jekyll?
4 . . . did Dr Jekyll take the drug again after two months without it?
5 . . . did Dr Jekyll have to ask Dr Lanyon for help?
6 . . . did Dr Jekyll become afraid of going to sleep?
7 . . . did Hyde need the hiding-place of Jekyll's body?
8 . . . couldn't Jekyll make his drug with new chemicals?

After Reading

1 **Complete this passage about Dr Jekyll, using some of the words below. Then write a passage about Mr Hyde, using the words which are left.**

criminal, cruel, disliked, doctor, evil, fear, generous, good, handsome, hate, horror, irresponsible, jealousy, kindly, liked, lost, serious, short, stronger, studious, tall, took, ugly, violent, weaker, wild

Dr Jekyll was _____, with a _____, _____ face. He was a _____, who lived a _____, _____ life, and people _____ him because he was a _____ and _____ man. As his character became _____, his feelings of _____ and _____ towards Hyde grew greater, and in the end he _____ control of him.

2 **What experience did the different people in the story have of Mr Hyde? Fill in the gaps with the right names.**

1   _____ was _____'s friend and cousin. He met _____ one winter's night, when _____ hurt a child in the street. He then saw _____ let himself into the mysterious building and come out with a cheque with _____'s name on it.

2   _____ was _____'s servant. He was afraid that _____ had murdered _____ and was in _____'s study. He fetched _____, and the two men broke into the study and found the body of _____.

3 _____ was an old friend of _____. He saw _____ only once, when he came to his house to collect some chemicals, and changed into _____ in front of his very eyes.

4 _____ was a lawyer. He knew _____'s name from _____'s will, and he once met _____ near _____'s house. The next time he saw him, _____ was lying dead in _____'s study.

3 **Dr Jekyll talked to Dr Lanyon about his ideas. Write out their conversation in the correct order and put in the speakers' names. Dr Lanyon speaks first (number 5).**

1 _____ 'No, not at all. I'm perfectly happy as I am.'

2 _____ 'By taking a drug which I have made.'

3 _____ 'I'm working on a rather exciting idea – something that will change all our lives, and make us free!'

4 _____ 'And how, exactly, do you plan to do that?'

5 _____ 'Well, Jekyll, I haven't seen you for weeks. What's made you so busy?'

6 _____ 'I don't want to discuss this. I think you must be mad, Jekyll. Go away and do something sensible.'

7 _____ 'Well, I'm not. And soon I shall be able to give each side of my character its own separate face and body.'

8 _____ 'A drug? This is imaginative rubbish, Jekyll. Completely unscientific, and a dangerous idea, too.'

9 _____ 'Haven't you ever wanted to separate the two sides of your character, and change from one to the other?'

10 _____ 'Nonsense, Lanyon. It's a wonderful idea. People will be able to enjoy two quite different lives.'

11 _____ 'Free? What on earth are you talking about, Jekyll?'

4 The letters from Dr Jekyll and Dr Lanyon were very strange, so Mr Utterson thought of an explanation that the police would believe. Complete his conversation with the police. (Use as many words as you like.)

POLICE: What did you find when you broke into the study?

MR UTTERSON: I found _____.

POLICE: You say that Mr Hyde is wearing Dr Jekyll's clothes. What do you think has happened to Dr Jekyll?

MR UTTERSON: I think _____.

POLICE: But where's the body? What did he do with it?

MR UTTERSON: Perhaps he _____.

POLICE: But then he stayed here in the study. Why?

MR UTTERSON: I think he was looking for _____.

POLICE: Why would he want to destroy Dr Jekyll's will?

MR UTTERSON: Because _____ and there _____.

POLICE: Mm. I see. And why did he kill himself?

MR UTTERSON: He was trapped in the study and he knew that _____.

POLICE: Well, if all this is true, the world has lost a good man and an evil one. Thank you for your help, Mr Utterson.

5 Complete these two newspaper reports about Dr Jekyll and Mr Hyde. (Use one word in each gap.)

Police were called late _____ night to the home _____ Dr Jekyll. The doctor's _____, Mr Utterson, and his _____ Poole had discovered the _____ of Edward Hyde in _____ doctor's study. Hyde, who _____ killed himself by taking _____, was wanted for the _____ of Sir Danvers Carew.

Police in London are _____ for the body of _____ scientist Dr
Henry Jekyll, _____ has now been missing _____ several days.
They believe _____ the doctor has been _____ by Mr Edward
Hyde, _____ body, dressed in clothes _____ belonged to the
doctor, _____ found last night, lying _____ Dr Jekyll's study.

Now write a suitable headline for each report.

6 **Here are some other titles for this story. Some are better than
others. Can you explain why? Think of some more titles of
your own.**

The Two Sides of Doctor Jekyll
The Battle between Good and Evil
Who Killed Dr Jekyll?
Evil Always Wins
The Strange Tale of Mr Utterson
Play with Life, Play with Death

7 **Do you agree (A) or disagree (D) with these sentences? Explain
why.**

1 Everybody has two sides to their character.
2 One side of a person's character is always evil.
3 People don't usually have a side to their character as evil as
   Mr Hyde, but most of us do some things in our lives that
   we are ashamed of.
4 Scientific experiments on animals and plants are all right,
   but experiments on people are wrong.

ABOUT THE AUTHOR

Robert Louis Stevenson was born in Edinburgh, in Scotland, in 1850. His father was an engineer, and in 1867 Robert went to Edinburgh University to study engineering himself. However, he soon found that engineering did not interest him. He trained to be a lawyer instead, but in fact he had already decided to be a writer. He met his future wife, Fanny Osbourne, in France. She was American, ten years older than Stevenson, and a married woman with two children. They fell in love, and after Fanny's divorce, she and Stevenson were married in 1880, in San Francisco in the USA.

Stevenson liked to travel, although much of the time his health was poor. In 1888, he and Fanny went to live on the Pacific island of Samoa because the weather there was good for Stevenson's health. The islanders called him 'The Teller of Tales'. He died on Samoa in 1894.

Stevenson wrote travel books, short stories, essays, and novels. His exciting adventure stories, such as *Treasure Island* (1883) and *Kidnapped* (1886), have been popular since they first appeared. *Dr Jekyll and Mr Hyde* (1886), another of his famous titles, became a popular play and has also been filmed many times. The kindly Dr Jekyll and the evil Mr Hyde have been played by such famous actors as John Barrymore, Bela Lugosi, Fredric March (who won an Oscar for it), Spencer Tracy, and Christopher Lee. The phrase 'Jekyll and Hyde', meaning someone with two very different sides to their personality, has become part of the English language.

ABOUT BOOKWORMS

OXFORD BOOKWORMS LIBRARY
Classics • True Stories • Fantasy & Horror • Human Interest
Crime & Mystery • Thriller & Adventure

The OXFORD BOOKWORMS LIBRARY offers a wide range of original and adapted stories, both classic and modern, which take learners from elementary to advanced level through six carefully graded language stages:

Stage 1 (400 headwords)	**Stage 4** (1400 headwords)
Stage 2 (700 headwords)	**Stage 5** (1800 headwords)
Stage 3 (1000 headwords)	**Stage 6** (2500 headwords)

More than fifty titles are also available on cassette, and there are many titles at Stages 1 to 4 which are specially recommended for younger learners. In addition to the introductions and activities in each Bookworm, resource material includes photocopiable test worksheets and Teacher's Handbooks, which contain advice on running a class library and using cassettes, and the answers for the activities in the books.

Several other series are linked to the OXFORD BOOKWORMS LIBRARY. They range from highly illustrated readers for young learners, to playscripts, non-fiction readers, and unsimplified texts for advanced learners.

Oxford Bookworms Starters	*Oxford Bookworms Factfiles*
Oxford Bookworms Playscripts	*Oxford Bookworms Collection*

Details of these series and a full list of all titles in the OXFORD BOOKWORMS LIBRARY can be found in the *Oxford English* catalogues. A selection of titles from the OXFORD BOOKWORMS LIBRARY can be found on the next pages.

BOOKWORMS · FANTASY & HORROR · STAGE 4

The Unquiet Grave

M. R. JAMES

Retold by Peter Hawkins

If you find a locked room in a lonely inn, don't try to open it, even on a bright sunny day. If you find a strange whistle hidden among the stones of an old church, don't blow it. If a mysterious man gives you a piece of paper with strange writing on it, give it back to him at once. And if you call a dead man from his grave, don't expect to sleep peacefully ever again.

Read these five ghost stories by daylight, and make sure your door is locked.

BOOKWORMS · FANTASY & HORROR · STAGE 4

The Whispering Knights

PENELOPE LIVELY

Retold by Clare West

'I don't know that you have done anything wrong,' Miss Hepplewhite said. 'But it is possible that you have done something rather dangerous.'

William and Susie thought they were just playing a game when they cooked a witch's brew in the old barn and said a spell over it, but Martha was not so sure. And indeed, the three friends soon learn that they have called up something dark and evil out of the distant past . . .

Treasure Island
ROBERT LOUIS STEVENSON

Retold by John Escott

'Suddenly, there was a high voice screaming in the darkness: "Pieces of eight! Pieces of eight! Pieces of eight!" It was Long John Silver's parrot, Captain Flint! I turned to run . . .'

But young Jim Hawkins does not escape from the pirates this time. Will he and his friends find the treasure before the pirates do? Will they escape from the island, and sail back to England with a ship full of gold?

The Songs of Distant Earth and Other Stories
ARTHUR C. CLARKE

Retold by Jennifer Bassett

'High above them, Lora and Clyde heard a sound their world had not heard for centuries – the thin scream of a starship coming in from outer space, leaving a long white tail like smoke across the clear blue sky. They looked at each other in wonder. After three hundred years of silence, Earth had reached out once more to touch Thalassa . . .'

And with the starship comes knowledge, and love, and pain.

In these five science-fiction stories Arthur C. Clarke takes us travelling through the universe into the unknown but always possible future.

Gulliver's Travels

JONATHAN SWIFT

Retold by Clare West

'Soon I felt something alive moving along my leg and up my body to my face, and when I looked down, I saw a very small human being, only fifteen centimetres tall . . . I was so surprised that I gave a great shout.'

But that is only the first of many surprises which Gulliver has on his travels. He visits a land of giants and a flying island, meets ghosts from the past and horses which talk . . .

Do Androids Dream of Electric Sheep?

PHILIP K. DICK

Retold by Andy Hopkins and Joc Potter

San Francisco lies under a cloud of radioactive dust. People live in half-deserted apartment buildings, and keep electric animals as pets because so many real animals have died. Most people emigrate to Mars – unless they have a job to do on Earth.

Like Rick Deckard – android killer for the police and owner of an electric sheep. This week he has to find, identify, and kill six androids which have escaped from Mars. They're machines, but they look and sound and think like humans – clever, dangerous humans. They will be hard to kill.

The film *Bladerunner* was based on this famous novel.